Lyle Ashton Harris

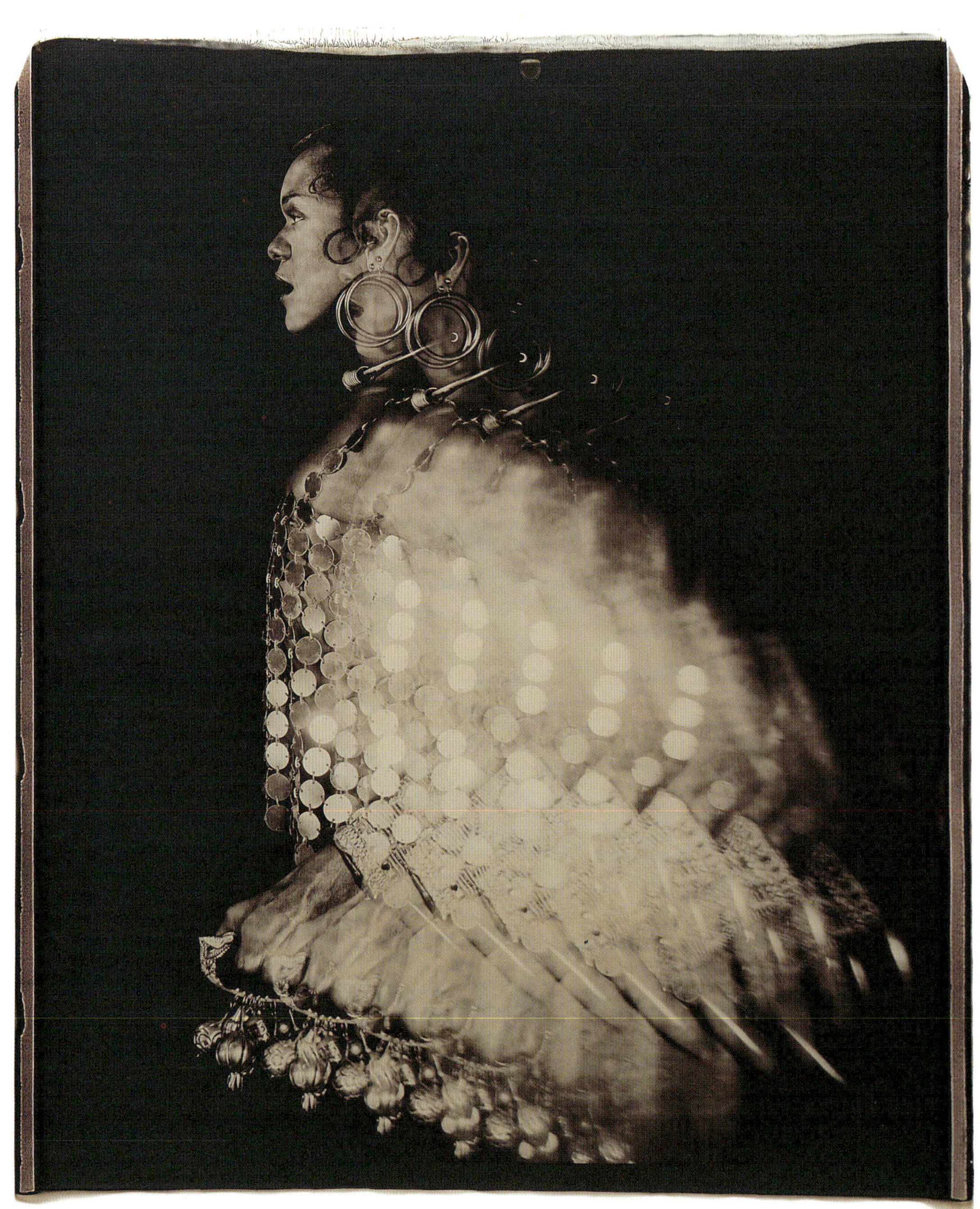

LYLE ASHTON HARRIS

WITH AN ESSAY BY

Anna Deavere Smith

GREGORY R. MILLER & COMPANY

IN COLLABORATION WITH

CRG Gallery, New York

[Billie] Holiday sometimes did more than just change
the emphasis of a song's meaning. At times she would use
her composer's capacity to change the song's meaning
to the opposite of what the original composer had in mind.

From *Lady Day: The Many Faces of Billie Holiday* by Robert G. O'Meally

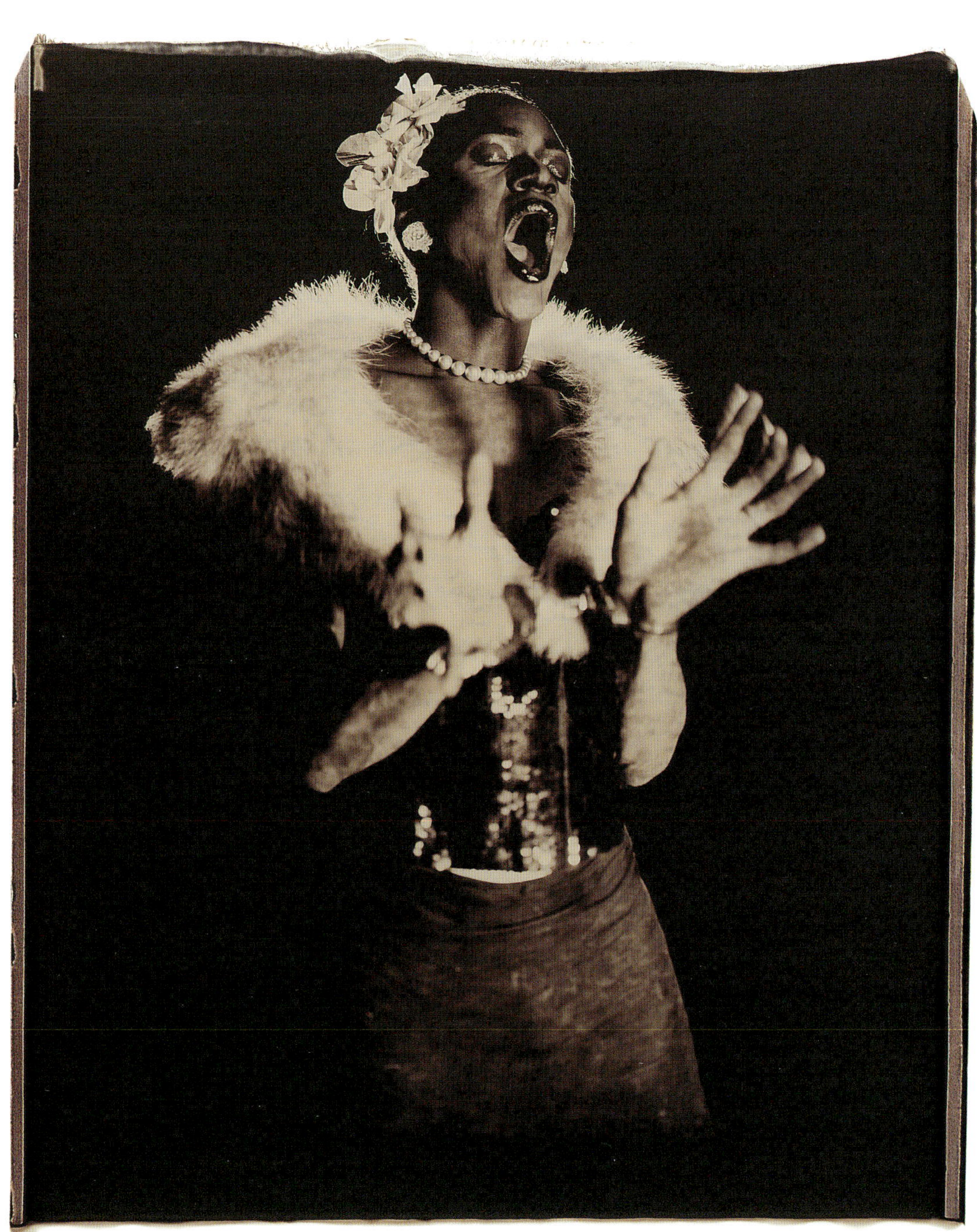

I

Lyle understands masculinity as performance, a fragile performance.

I suspect he understands femininity similarly.

He dares to play with that in relation to the black male body,

    which has been declared endangered for some time now.

Lyle's work questions the meaning of maleness and femaleness,

        not to mention blackness and whiteness.

He changes it to something that is very

            different

                from what the "composer" had in mind.

Is it possible that, now, we can look at identity as a constellation:

    that each of us has inside of ourselves many fragments?

            And the fragments are not neurosis.

Our work, in our societies, as human beings, as linguistic animals, is to find a way

    to give each part its movement

           in the wondrous constellation that is our humanity.

Like the music of the spheres.

        Not as a fixed, reiterated performance,

          but as an improvisation.

              As jazz.

If you know Lyle, you know that he says a lot of words very quickly.

One such string of words was,

"A sissy by five,

a faggot by seven,

a bitch by twelve,

a cunt by eighteen.

These were all called to me."

He tells me that it was extremely hurtful to have "sissy" hurled at him,

and to have "faggot" hurled at him.

"I took it personally," he told me, but—and here is the clincher—he said,

"It was not an assault on my masculinity."

At first I thought I was lookin' *at* Lyle

And now I know I am lookin' *for* Lyle.

He will never let me look at him

Because the moment I think I see him

He will conclude his run-on sentence.

And when he does conclude his run-on then there are no words

And in the silence,

he looks at me

And the gaze is so strong

I have to look   away.

Is he looking for a mirror in me,

or am I looking for one in him?

II

Sugar. Lyle is haunted by Sugar.

Sugar is an inspiration for the photographs of himself as Billie and himself as the boxer.

Sugar was a cousin of Lyle's who cross-dressed. Sugar ended up dead in the gutter
for his transgressions. Lyle's grandfather had to come down to New York City
to identify Sugar's body.

Sugar did the ultimate transgression,

a transgression that Lyle cannot do.

Yes, Lyle can photograph himself

in a blond wig and crinoline,

exposing his own genitals for all the world to see.

But all of those transgressions are in the safety of his studio, in the safety of a presumed metaphor,
in the safety of the place where

the artist, who plays the fool for society,

resides. And you see,
the fool historically has been able to say things that everyone else would be shot for saying.

The fool tells the truth.

Sugar was trying to tell a truth, I think. And he died for it.

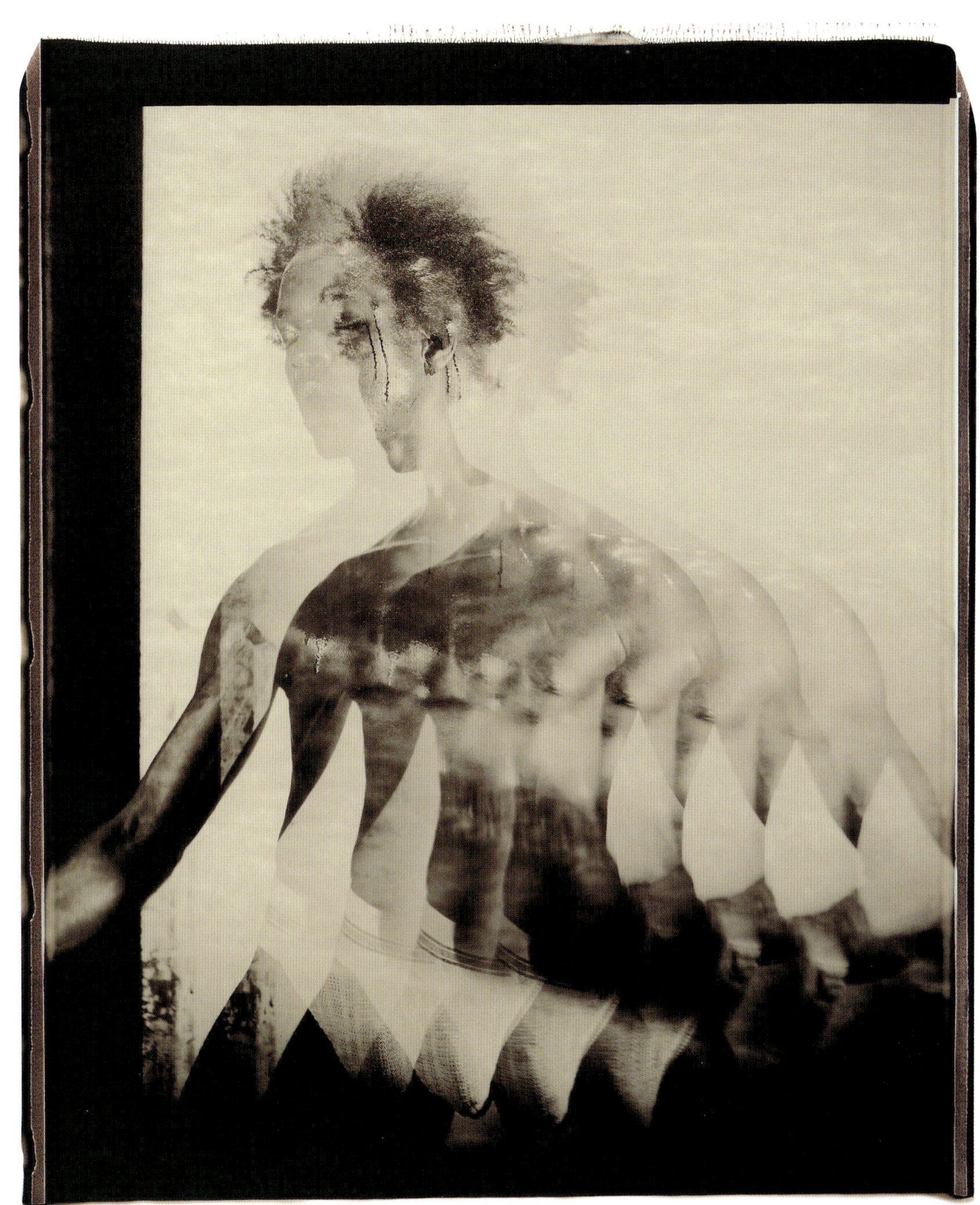

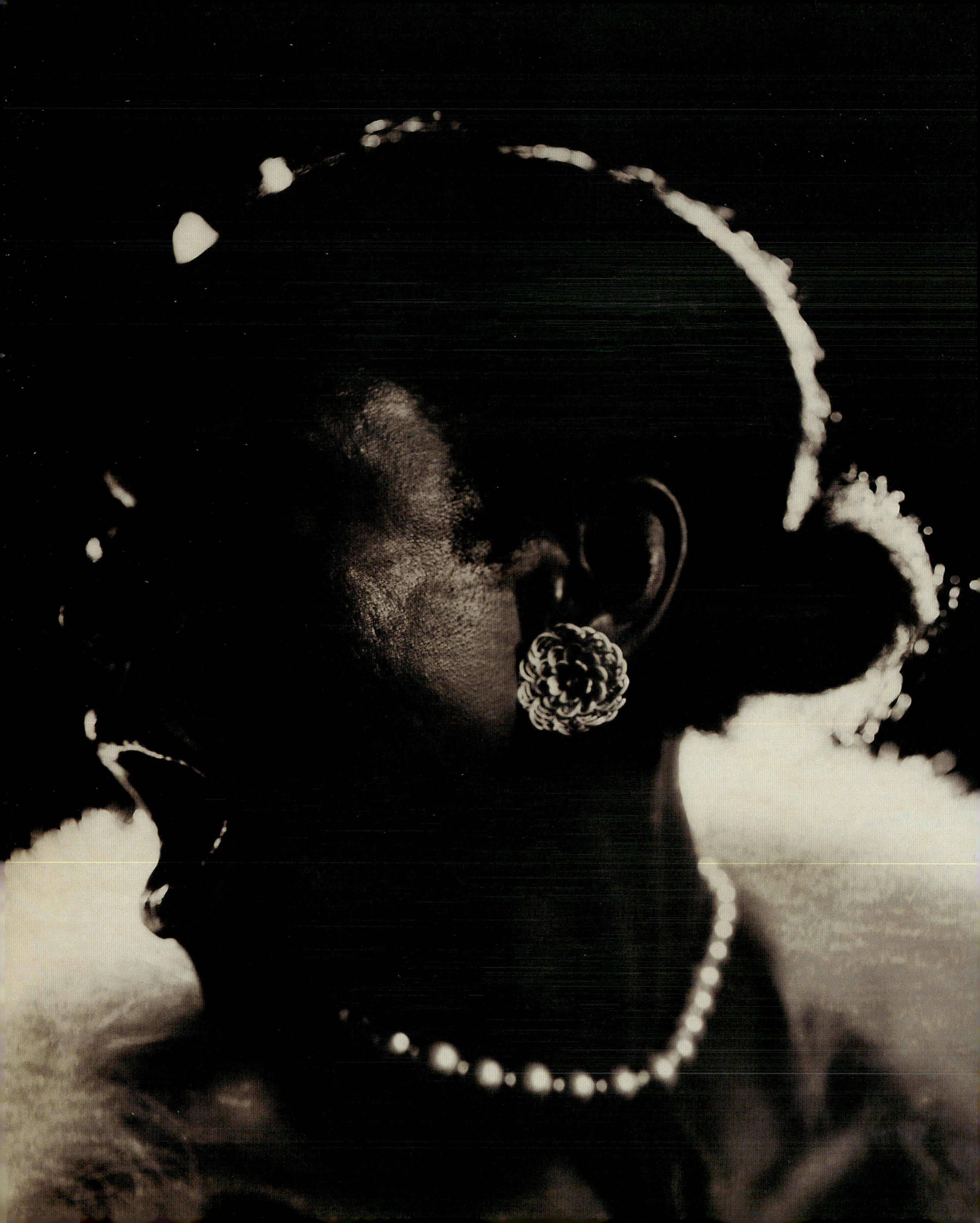

III

The Better Days Bar is where Lyle was called "cunt" at age seventeen or eighteen.
        He was going there around the time he was about to enter Wesleyan University.

The Better Days Bar was a dive on West 44th or West 47th Street
        frequented by black and latino men,
                                and the white guys who were into them.

        He went there lookin' for Daddy.

The Better Days Bar is the type of establishment that Sugar would have frequented.
    Since Lyle is haunted by Sugar,
                I wonder if he went there
                                lookin' not only for Daddy,
                                        but for Sugar.

IV

The first time I laid eyes on this work, I asked him,
        "What does it mean that you are playing Billie Holiday on the one hand,
                                            and a boxer on the other?"
And he said,
            not confrontationally,
                    but with that look of surprise and readiness to engage on his face,
                        "Well, what do you think?"

Lyle is in a transition.   He is not here,   he is not there,
            he is   in between
                        here   and   there.

        He is looking for something more in himself.

        That which haunts him about Sugar
            is that which he longs for:
                                    the sacrifice.
            To shed anything that keeps him at bay.

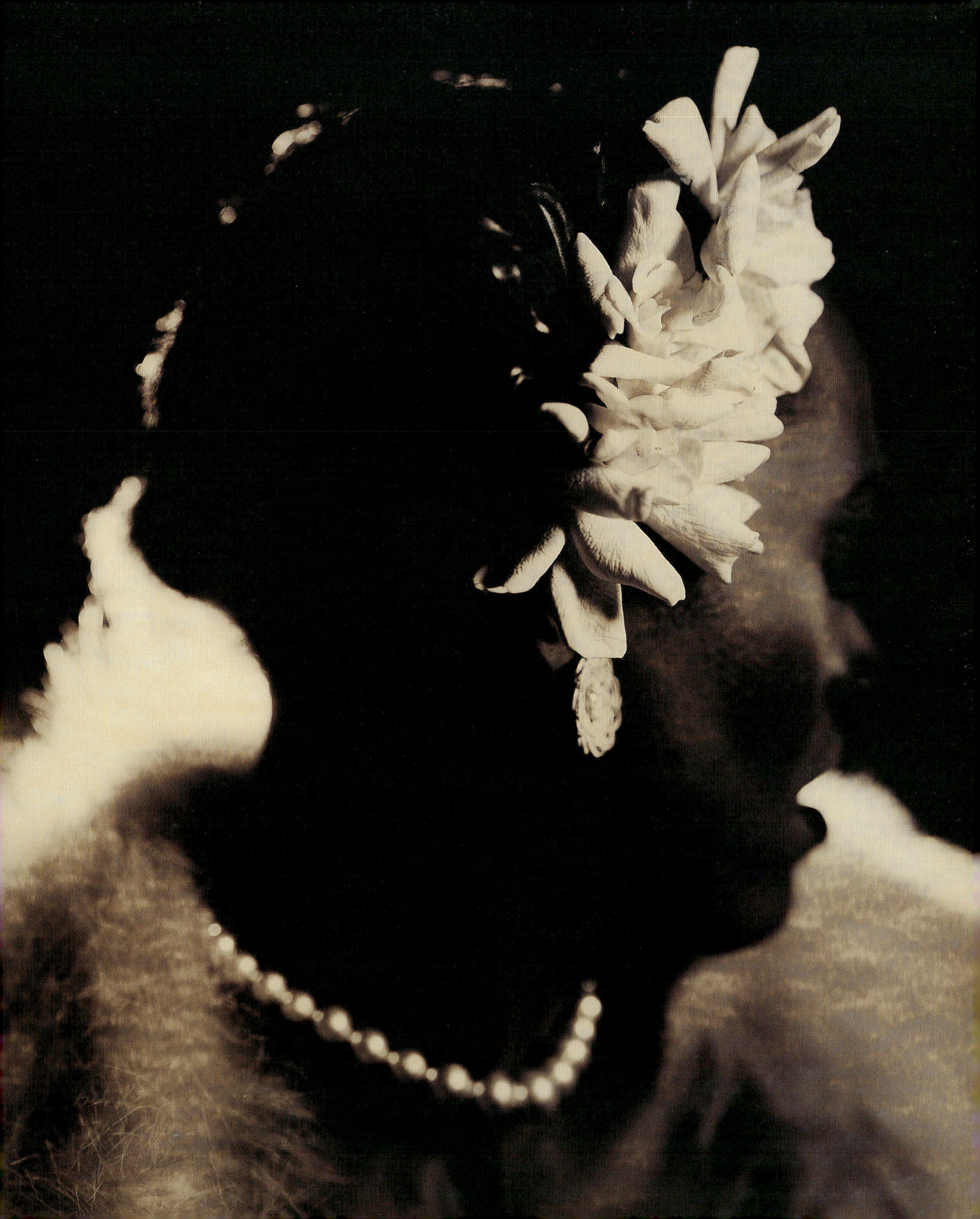

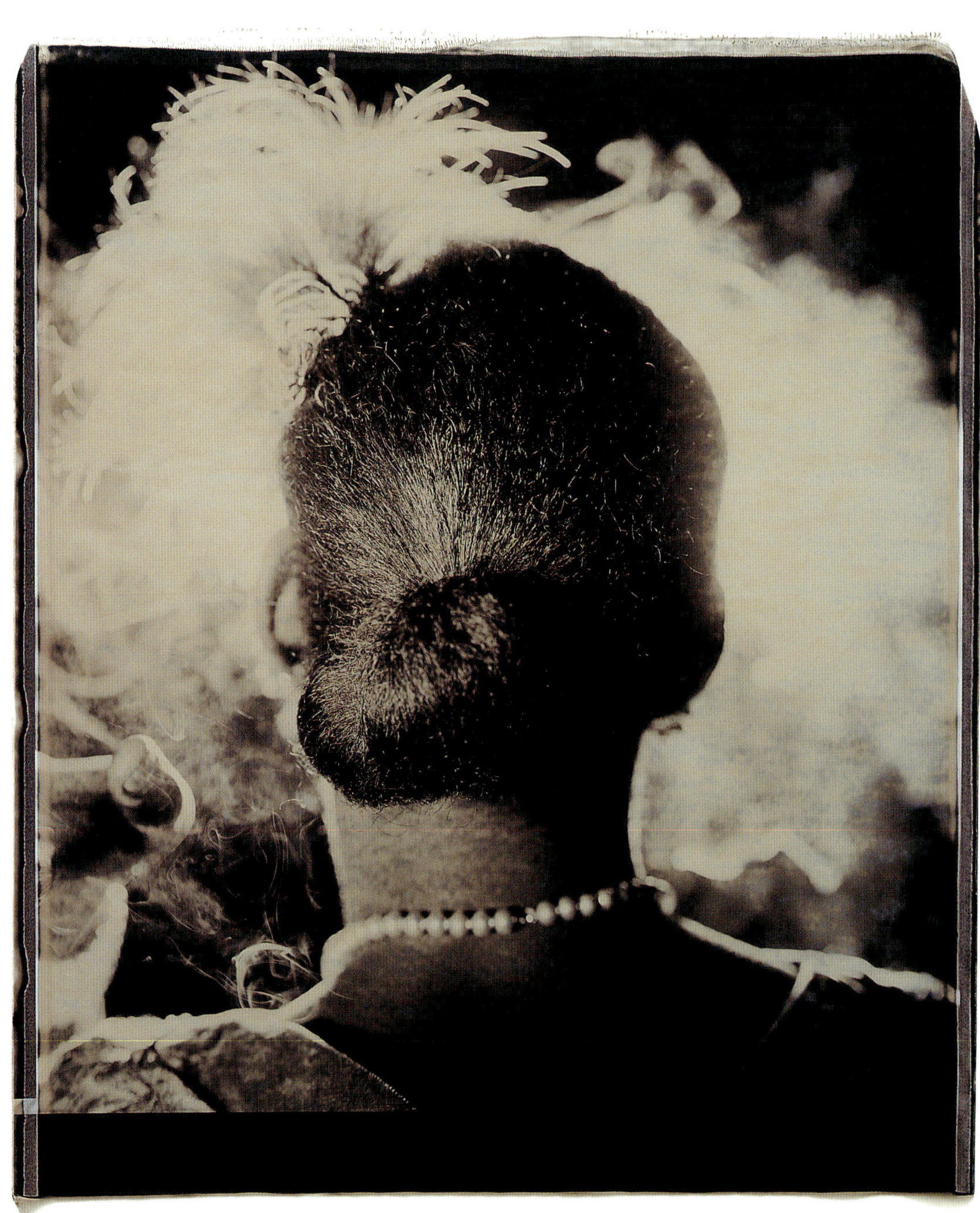

That which entrances him and haunts him about Billie Holiday

is that which he longs for:

the sacrifice.

He is interested in her addictions.

He is interested in how far Billie went.

He would like to go that far.

I asked him what he would have to risk to go so far?

He told me.

But I would never presume to interpret it for you.

I will list exactly what he told me.

"Exposure."

"Seduction, I would have to risk seduction."

"I would have to give up the illusion of desire."

"I am ready to tell a story of recovery."

"Death is on the horizon."

I know what I think Lyle would have to risk.

He would have to risk touching the loss in black life.

It's hard to touch the loss.

But Lyle is trying to touch it.

V

The first time I asked Lyle about his recovery (because he had used the word a lot)
he was not so generous with his words.
I had to pry.   I don't like to pry.   "Do you drink?"
"No, I don't drink," he said quickly.
Just as quickly, he said he does not do drugs anymore,
and then he shut down the interaction by saying he had other addictions.
And it wasn't rude, the way he shut it down, but it put me in touch with my own search
for "Daddy."
I felt as though,
perhaps,
if he were to tell me of his addictions,
I wouldn't "get it,"
or that it was none of my business.   He smiled,
and looked away.
Not shyly. Perhaps a little slyly.

Like maybe, one day, if I were good, I would find out.
You see,
we are all looking for Daddy,
and we might not even know it.
As for me,
I am looking for Daddy too, with Daddy being the ultimate authority on knowledge,
the ultimate one who answers all the questions.

And for this moment,
when I could not get the answer
and I was sure that Lyle knew I was asking the question,
he was, for me,
that dark Daddy who does not give the answer and responds only in glances or riddles.

But recovery is something that you have to keep coming back to.
So one day I came back to Lyle with my question about his recovery,
and he said:
"It has been a long recovery."
"From drugs."
"From compulsive sex."
"Coming from a working middle-class background."
"My capacity to hurt."
"My capacity to dominate."
"And judge.""And be critical."
"And to be self-centered."
"And to be self-hating." I asked about risk again.
"I would risk not being loved.
I would re-experience being rejected, being left."

Beware if you think that this section has let all of Lyle's shit hang out.
If you think for a second that Lyle would ever let all of his shit hang out,
you are mistaken.

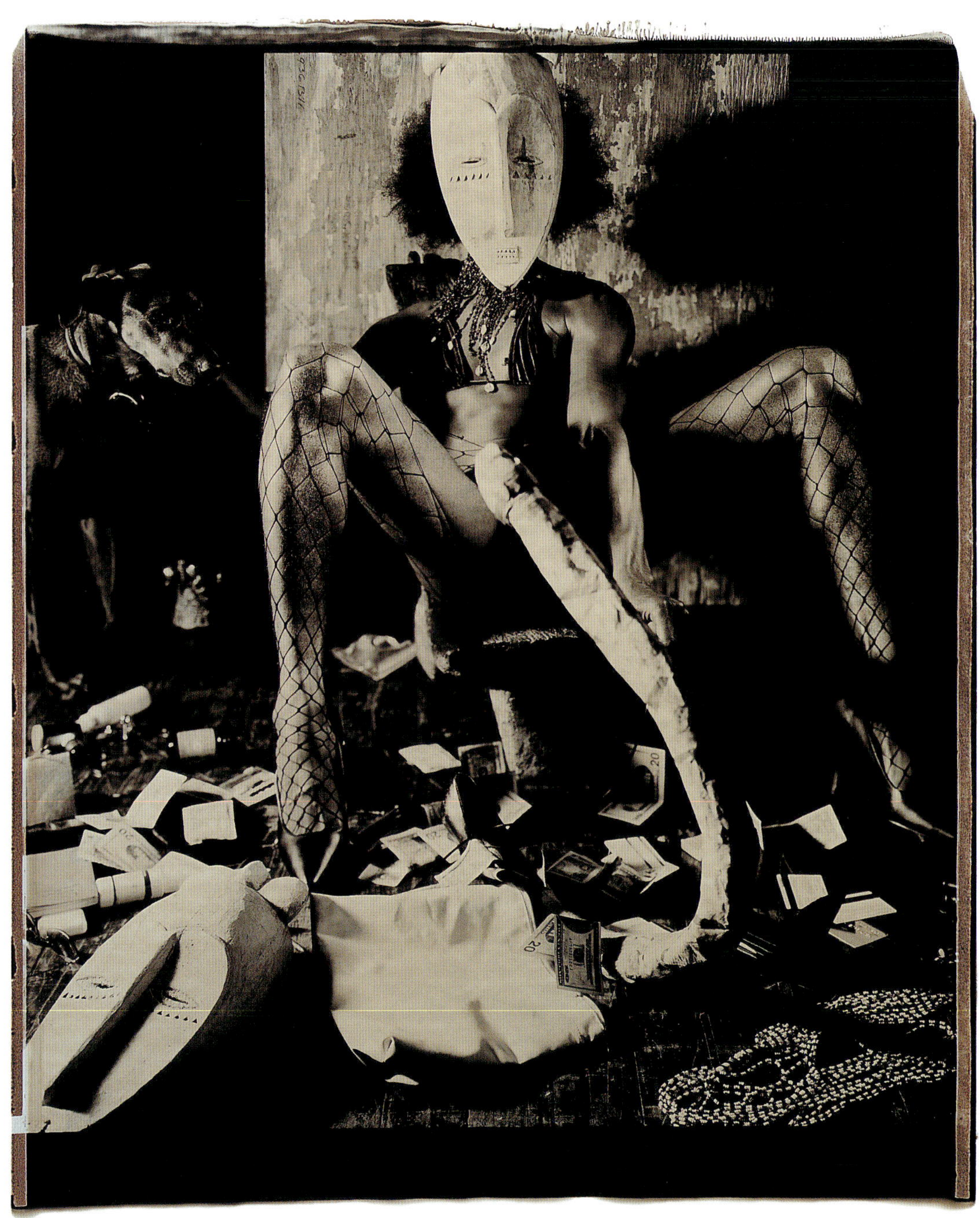

VI

When I went to Lyle's studio to see his new work
                              there was one photograph that I did not understand.
         It's the one where Lyle is seated in a chair with a mask on
              and his hair is protruding from each side of the mask.
                   His legs are very long and are stretched out.
They are covered in fishnet stockings. He is wearing high heels.
         An arm is draped over the chair and behind him is a dog. A rule of the theater is
                                                                    "no dogs or children,"
                                                                    the idea being
                                                                    that a dog or a child is so real
                                                                    that they will steal the scene.

              Yet, this scene has a dog, and it is still Lyle's scene.
       His "stuff"—twenty-dollar bills, items as if a woman's purse
       had been emptied during a robbery or a beating or a rape—
                                        is all over the floor.
                   A long papier-mâché phallus
                   designed by his friend Isabelle
              is coming down from his groin to the floor,
and the phallus is connected at the bottom to a woman's shoe.
       Behind the papier-mâché phallus are Lyle's own real genitals.
                             On the one hand, all of his shit is hanging out.
                   On the other hand,
                                   he is masked.

The mask sits on him in the picture

     the way he concludes a string of run-on sentences with a final simple sentence,

  and then is still for a moment.

And it would seem that with the final sentence you have heard everything,

    but in fact you have not heard everything.

    In fact you are just beginning to hear, and all you hear is the silence.

   And so he sits in the mask.

   And you are caused again to look at his shit all over the floor.

   And then, of course,

   Like the greedy audiences of Billie and the boxer, you want more.

   He has given it all to you and you have not seen enough.

   In your pursuit of all

   You are looking for the nothing.

   You are addicted.

   No matter how much he shows you

   You will want to see more

   And no matter how much he shows you

   There is a lot more stuff that he can keep to himself behind the mask.

  And then

   there is the dog, peering out at you,

       her eyes twinkling in the haunted hall of shit.

   Years ago, I read a book by Maya Deren, the filmmaker, on possession.

  The chapter on possession itself is called "White Lightning,"

and it's all about the absolute terror that comes moments before you are possessed.

      The possession itself is not terrifying.

     But the moment *before* possession is terrifying.

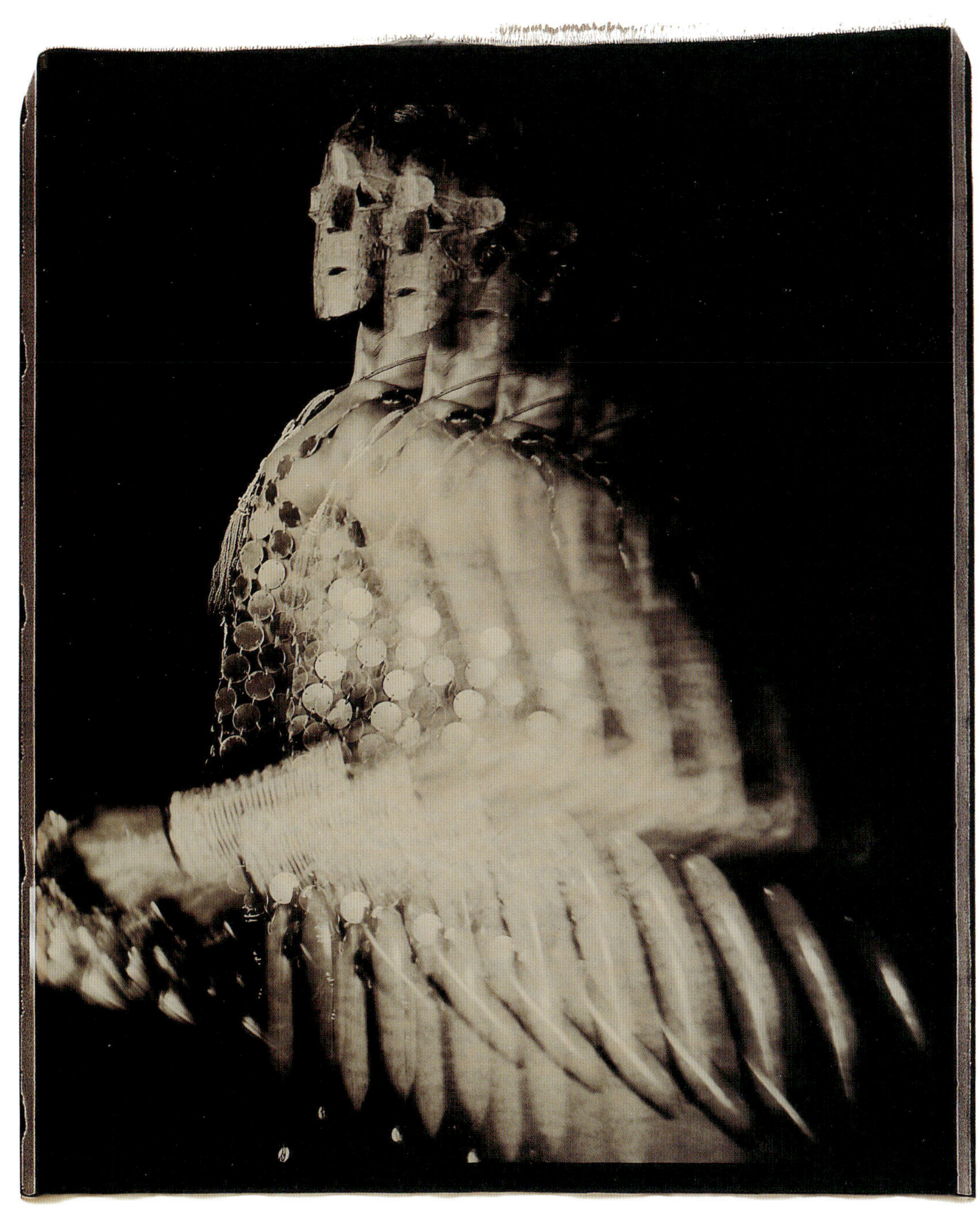

Lyle is self-possessed.

But the self is so diverse.

It is not just some boring personal testimony.

There is no such thing as the literal "personal" with Lyle.

The personal with Lyle is a dynamic.

It is an energy.

It is his pursuit.

It is not a list of facts.

It is not a biography.

It is not a narrative.

It is not a statement of who what when and where Lyle was.

Lyle is not just here and there.

He is between   here and there.   He always was.

Well, hell, wouldn't you be,

if you were called a sissy by five a faggot by seven,

to be perfectly tacky about the matter,

if I must be?

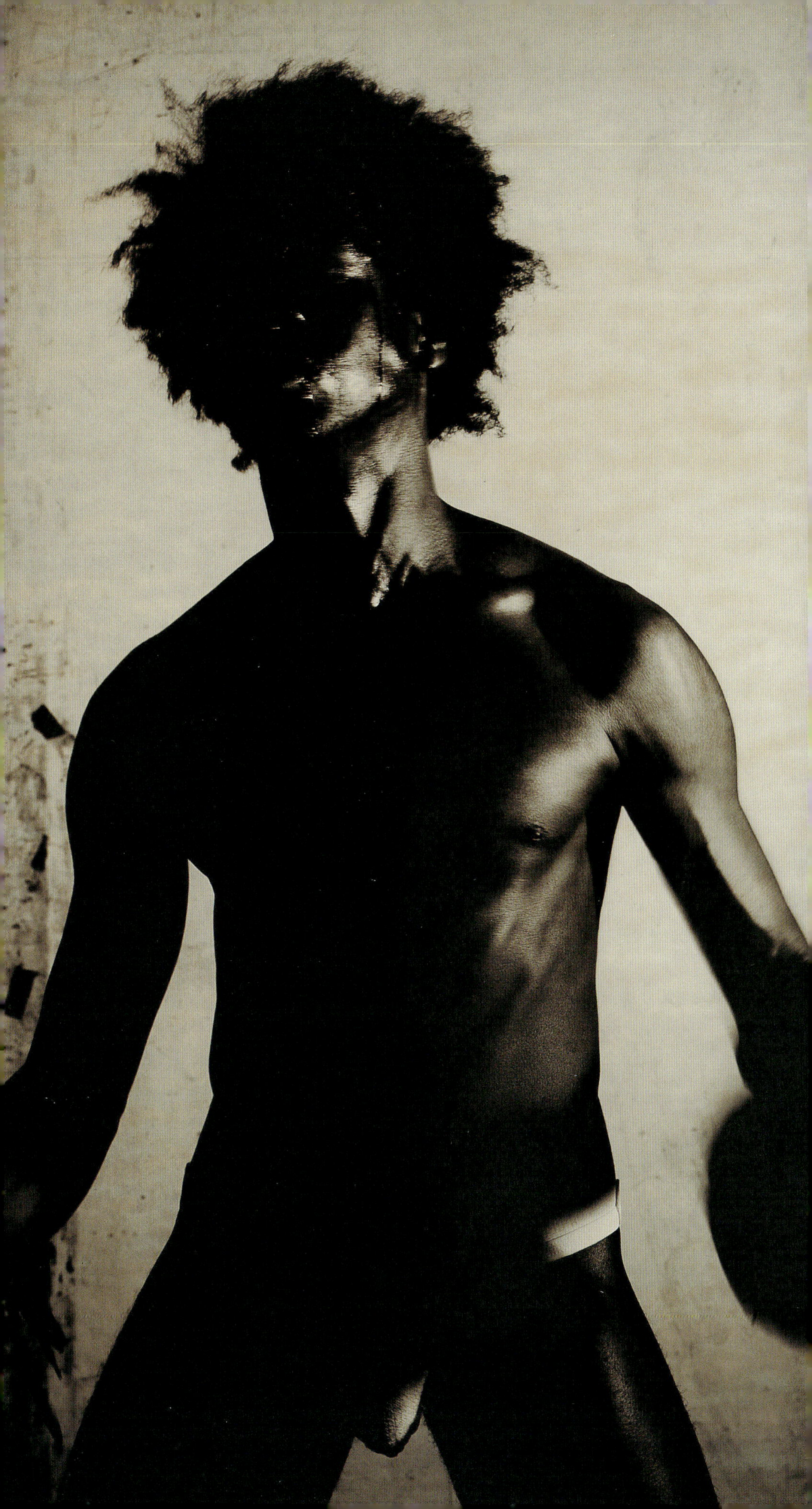

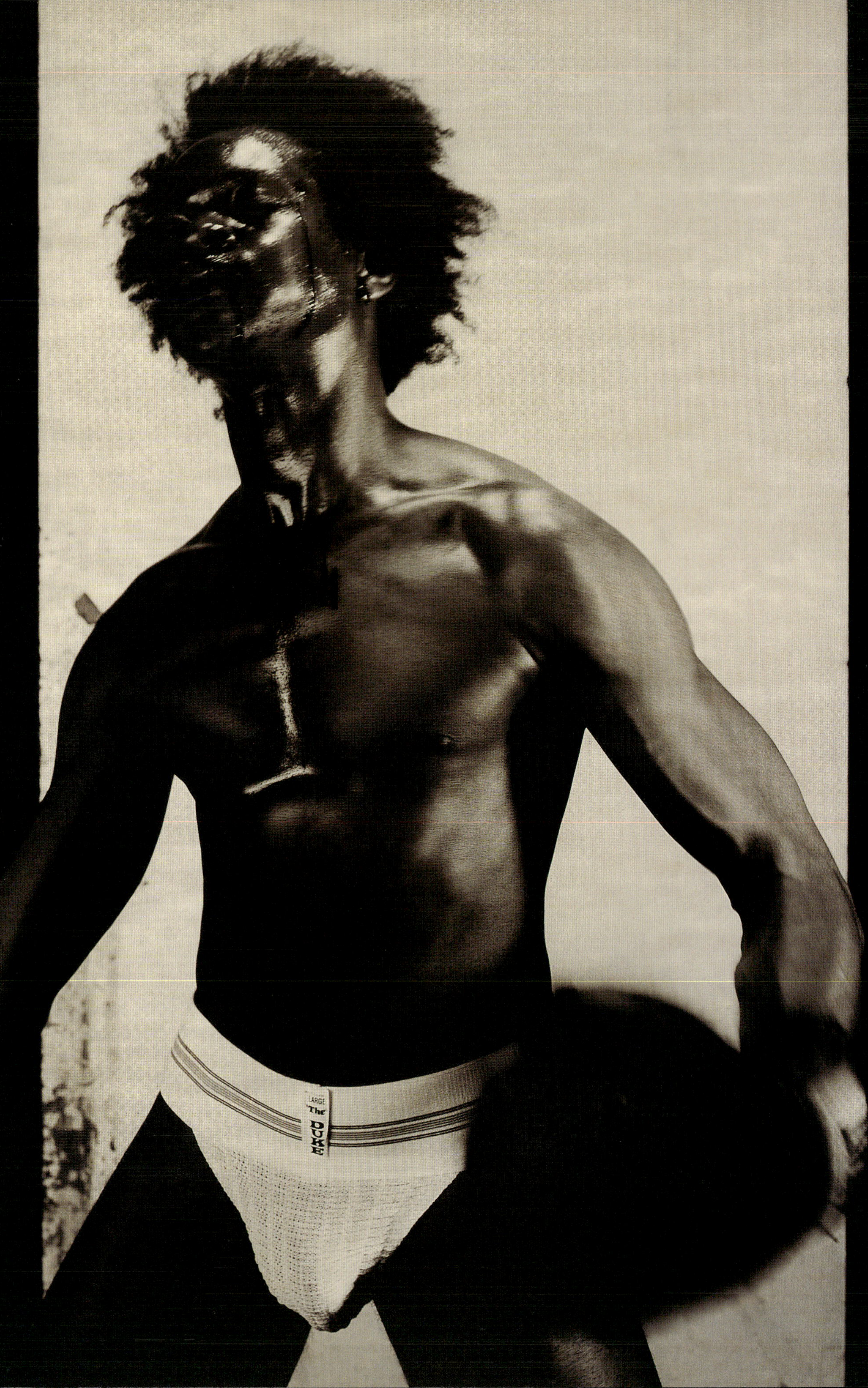

LARGE
The
DUKE

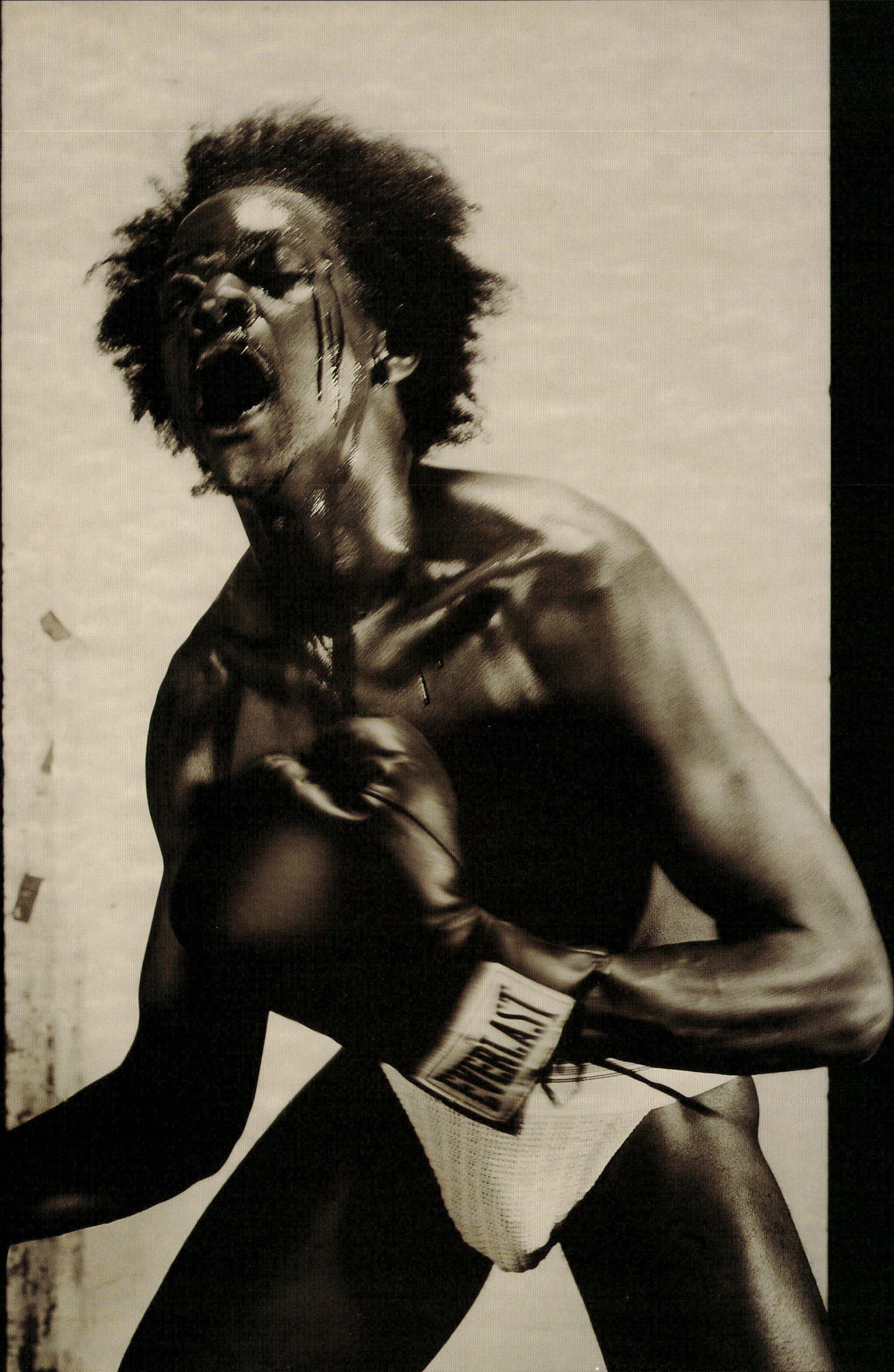
EVERLAST

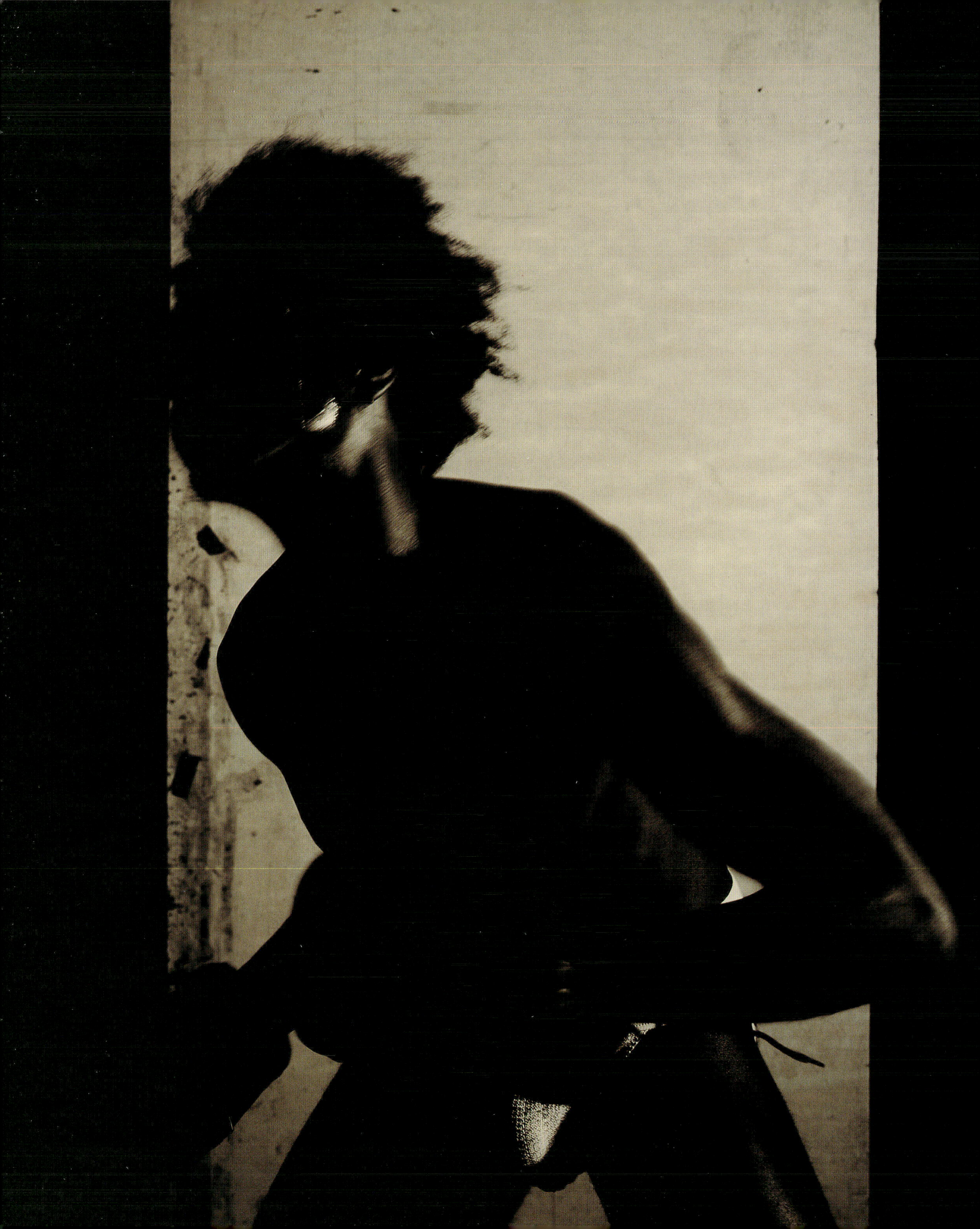

VII

When Lyle was young,
Christmas 1973 to be exact,
                  he and his mother and brother were at his aunt's house.
        His father,
           who had not been in touch for a year,   called.
            Lyle and his brother were excited   to talk to him.
  But his mother took the phone
             and told his father to just not bother to call
                if he wasn't going to call all year.
Lyle was disappointed and ashamed.
           Ashamed for wanting.
   He was longing for his Daddy and wanted to destroy that which he longed for.

But let's face it.
We live in a society that has been looking for Daddy.
              And no matter how badly he treated "us."
              At our jobs
              In our countries
              In our cities
              With our money
              With our health
              With our lives
    In relation to other countries in the world.
                   Why do we take it?

How could you deal with the recurring feeling of the embarrassment
and loss and things lost, or things broken, when you move from one
state of mind to another state of mind? And then you look back on
your old state of mind and you are surprised that the old state of
you was really you? And yet you know you lived in that state
for a long time, even if it was a state of "carceration"?

We have to sing about it
                         because there is no Mama
                          in our patriarchal culture,
            sitting in the throne next to the patriarch.

How come we don't have a Mama like Lyle's Mama
                who metaphorically goes to the phone
                              and tells our Daddies, just don't bother to call?

Billie Holiday was a Mama like that to her audience of babies lookin' for their Daddies.

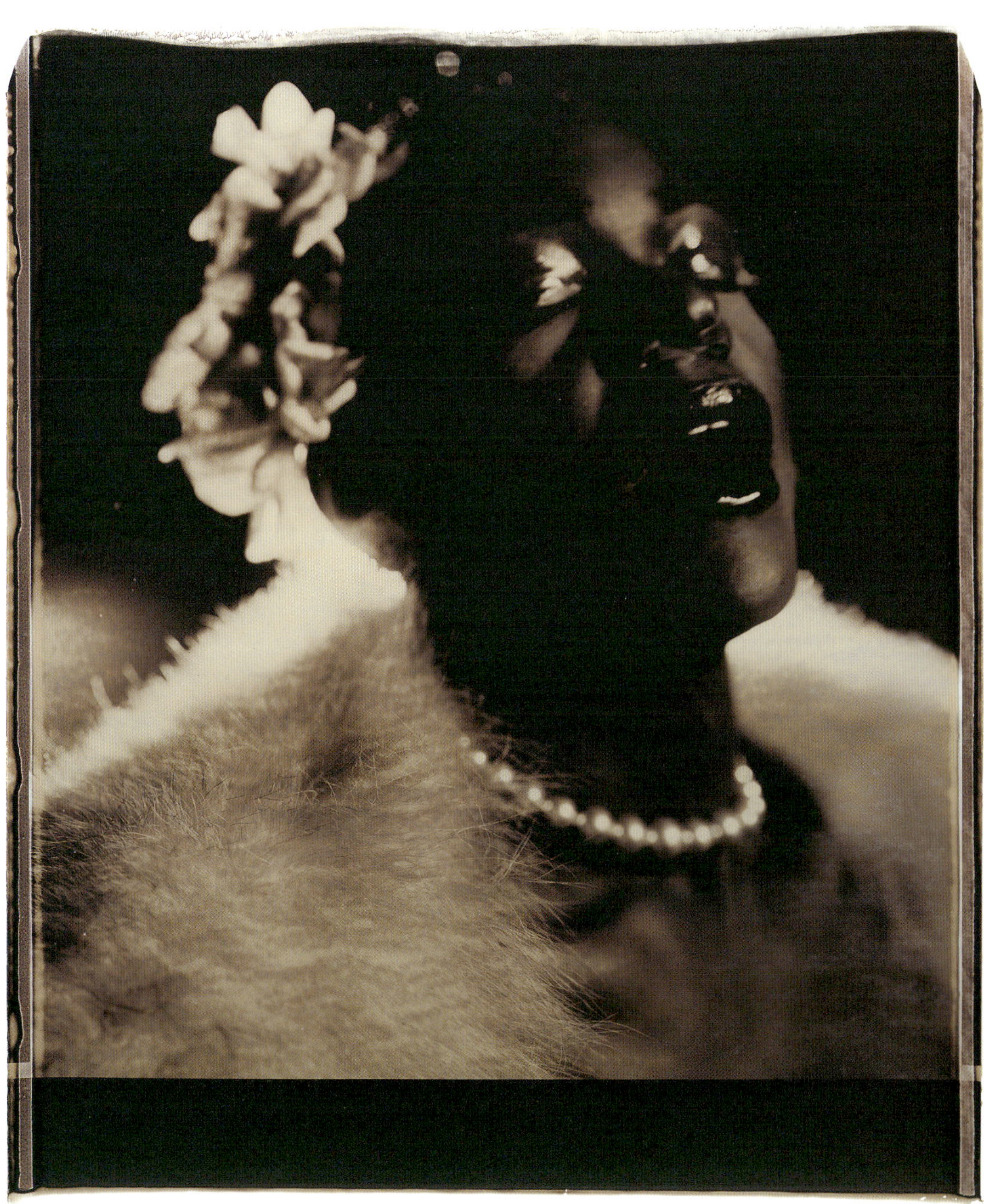

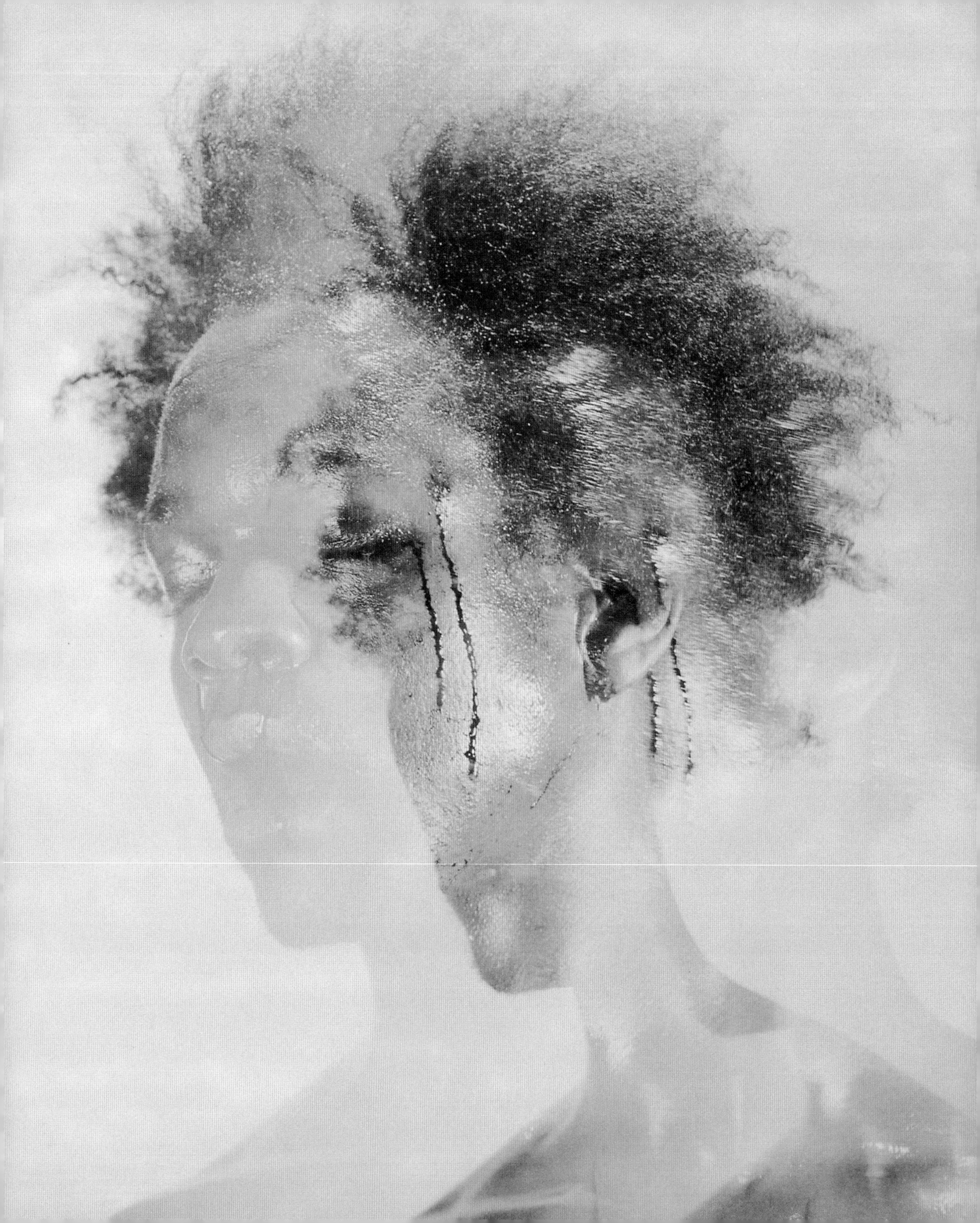

VIII

What I am about to tell you, you may already know—but I did not know this,
                so I will share it in the spirit of my coming from a state of knowing
                to a state of not knowing which is the only state where real knowledge is,
        that state between knowing   and not knowing,   and
                the state between not knowing   and knowing,
                that place where your brain clicks in.
I wanted to get beyond that state of presumptuous kinship with Lyle.   Even though
    I liked him by vibe,   I knew that I did not know him.   Even though
        I own three of his photographs.   Looking is one thing, knowing is another.

Lyle talks fast.   I am not the first to mention how he talks.
        He talks in what my mother,
                        a middle-class negro teacher woman in Baltimore,
                                would have called run-on sentences.
To some it's sentences, to me it's music.
                                And as far as I am concerned,
                                a sentence is an incarcerated idea.
                                    A sentence is a mask
        and I like the way his words spill out all over the sentence
    like blood on the boxer's face,
    or beauty on Billie's face.
        Or just like that picture where you think that all of Lyle's shit is hanging out
                because his dick and his twenty-dollar bills and . . . his hair is sticking out,
        and the fact of the basic Sugar in Lyle is right there in those fishnet stockings,
                                but in the end
                                    he is still masked.

Perhaps if there is any such thing as love at first sight,

then for me it was love at first hear—

the first time I heard Lyle talk.

I love the music of Lyle talking.

If I may—let me play a little Lyle for you—

on a Sunday afternoon the music of Lyle in his studio might have notes about—

his mother, his stepfather, Africa,

the failure of the heroic father,

the fragility of the male,

the experience of not being masculine,

of not being black enough,

"My Man," bruises, Louima, bruises,

highly charged sexualized acts,

that Christmas phone call from his Daddy,

beauty, Jeffrey Dahmer, bruises, Pulp Fiction,

Basquiat, Coltrane, Baldwin, Mohammed Ali, etcetera,

looking for Daddy,

"All of Me,"

the gorgeous sequence

about how his mother protected him

and finally I asked if he protected her

and he looked at me with that look of surprise

and he said succinctly and melodically, conclusively,

in that way that says it all

but does not give away all of his shit—

"We protected each *other*."

That was the final answer.   "Each *other*."

Emphasis on "*other*."

Lyle and his mother. Each *other*.

In coming to his studio, lookin' for Lyle, I would never expect to find answers, only questions.
And so "we protected each *other*" was the perfect answer

                                        that was not an answer but a full stop.

          Breath.

          Sugar, who cross-dressed in Albany and New York City in the 1950s,
          Sugar who died in the gutter,
                                        transgressions,
          "Blue Turning Grey Over You,"   beauty,
          Alice Miller, Drama of the Gifted Child,
the Better Days Bar, a dive for black men and latinos and the white men who were into them
                                                            (into them)
          Sugar, dead, in the gutter, "Strange Fruit"
                              a sissy by five a faggot a bitch a cunt,
                              all of these names were called to me, etcetera,
Billie, the singer of a troubled song is how the critics called her,
                    I think Lyle would call her Billie a singer of a beautiful song,
          Billie a singer of a sacrificial song,
                    a transgressive song,
                    a longing song,
                    addictions,
                    compulsions,
                    transgressions,
                    melancholy as the unfinished business of his mourning.
In the midst of one such fecund stringed instrument as Lyle's mind and mouth,
          a string of ideas—
                    if you will—
                              he said,
                              "And dealing with a fatal illness . . ."

He did not say "etcetera" at the conclusion of that phrase,
but it was almost as if he did,
his musical tone was as if it were a song he had sung many times.
Almost as if this is something I knew. But I didn't know.
He had not told me this the first time we met,
years ago, at George Wolfe's New Year's Day party
when he had introduced himself to me by saying
I reminded him of Adrian Piper.
He had not told me this
when I dedicated a performance to him
at the Santa Monica Museum of Art when Peter Norton invited me to perform there.
He did not include this fact in a note accompanying the photograph
that he sent to my flat in San Francisco,
a gift, a surprise—Coquette in white face
—that had adorned the top of my stairway for eight years
so no one could possibly miss it.
And he had not told me this
when he called out of the blue a couple years ago
and invited me to a party at Cindy Sherman's.
He did not mention the "fatal illness"
when I went to the Polaroid studio downtown
lookin' for something of his to shake up my clinically white-walled office.
I am not a scholar of Lyle so I had not read this fact.
So when he said,
"And dealing with a fatal illness,"
as if he were going to conclude the string with the rhythmic punctuation
that often punctuates his music
—that punctuation usually being "etcetera"
—I stopped him in his tracks.
It may even be that I stopped him
before he could say "etcetera."

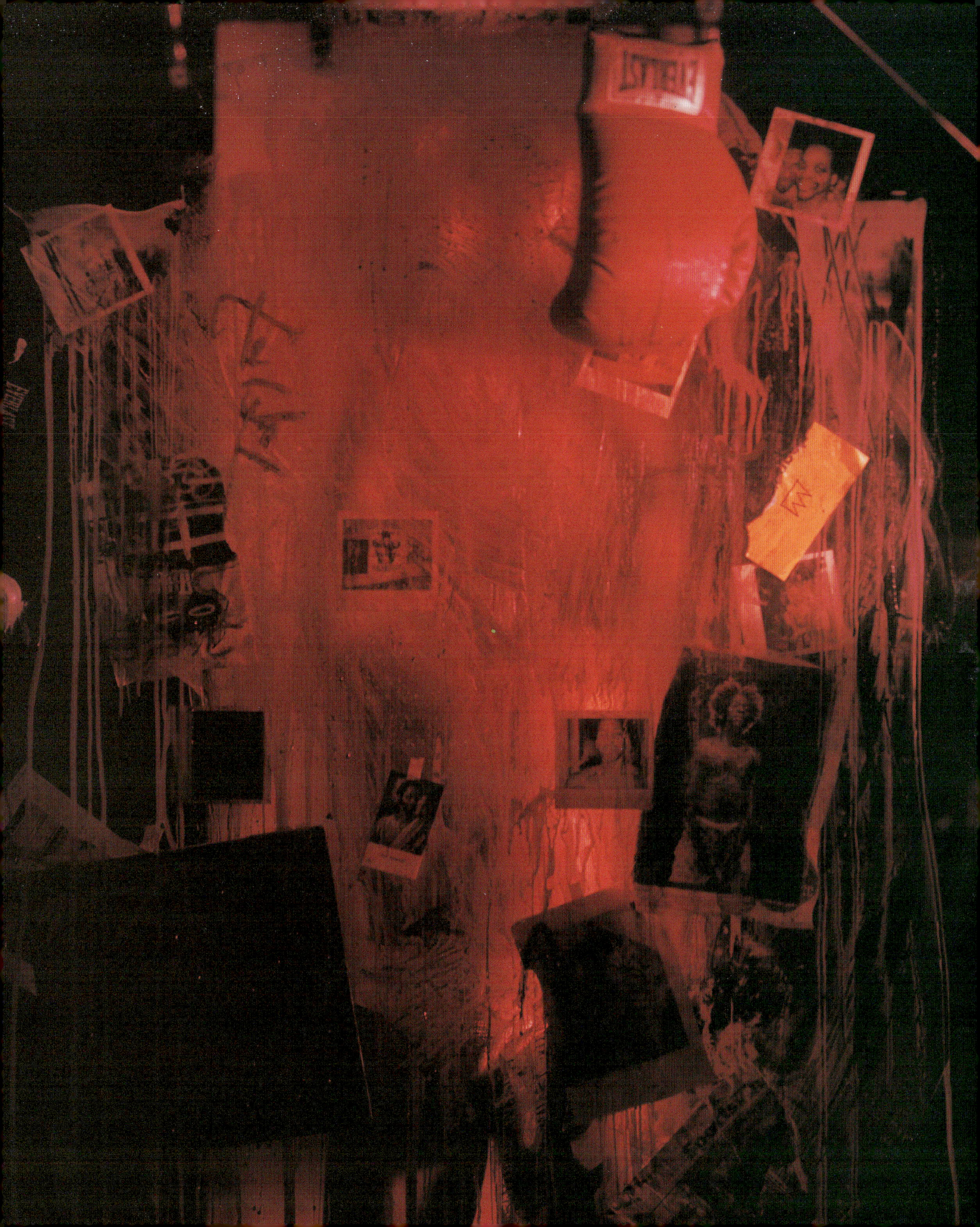
EVERLAST

I stopped him the way my Aunt Lorraine,

        a kind, middle-class, black teacher woman from Baltimore,

    would have stopped him.

Without making any visible rupture in the conversation.

Without stopping the flow of the music.

Never stopping, always under.

        Under what he was saying next, like a piano or a horn under a singer.

        Under

        (perhaps he would take it as another voice in his own consciousness),

      I said—

          "You have a fatal illness?"

    Swiftly, he said: "In '89, I was diagnosed with HIV.

          At twenty-two I was dealing with the possibility of death."

Over (perhaps over

any sadness or concern I might have),

      he said:

         "I've never been symptomatic.

         I've never had to take medication."

    And that was the end

      Of his answers

And the beginning of my unspoken questions.

      Once again.

As I say, he did not say etcetera,   In one of the books Lyle gave me,

   It was almost as if he did.   the author said

There is no etcetera about HIV.   Billie Holiday's voice was like a horn.

     Epidemic as it may be,   One time a saxophone player told me

each case should be named by   that the saxophone was the instrument

   its own name, and not by et   most like the human voice

      cet er a.   because it so depends on your breathing.

When Lyle gave me this information about his life,

      I heard a beautiful saxophone wailing.

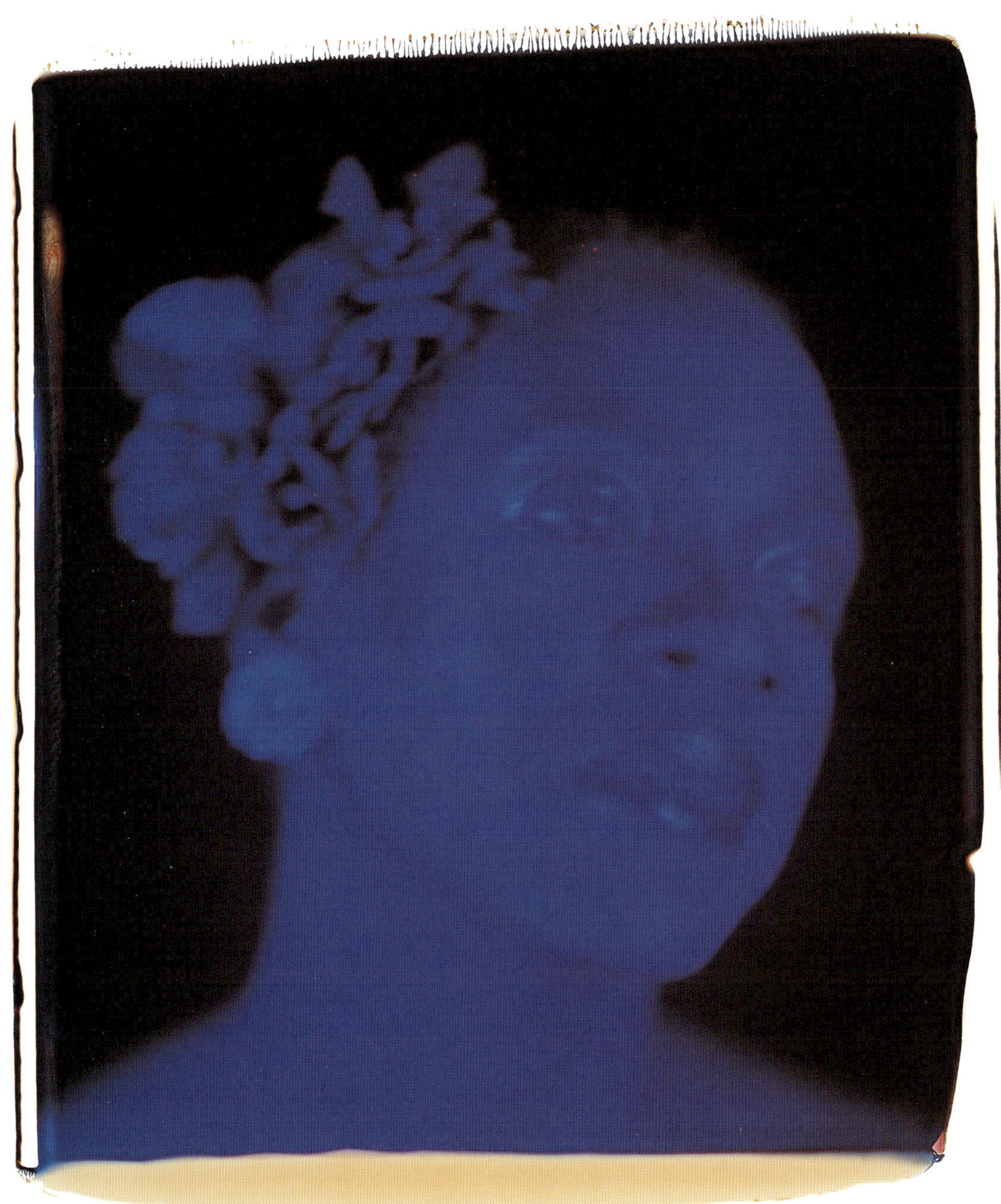

IX

I have been boxing for a year now, with a very good-looking testosterone kind of guy,
half Italian, half Puerto Rican, from Brooklyn, called Benny, who was a champ,
on his way to the Olympics, as a boxer.
                              He gave up the dream to take care of his son,
                                      because the Mama was a problem,
                                      and Benny had not had a Daddy,
                    so I guess he knew if he did not become a Daddy to his baby
                          then the baby would spend his life lookin' for Daddy,
                    so Benny became the Daddy
                                      instead of becoming the boxer.

        He answers all my questions.
              "What do women like?" I asked. He said,
                          "Women.
                          Women like to be held.
                          Women like to be kissed.
                          Women like you to be romantic.
                                      I am very romantic.
              I nevuh struck out on my first date.
                                      Nevuh.
                                      Nevuh."

And we moved around the gym
                    like we were dancing.
                                   "Upper cut, right hand."
                                                    (I flubbed.)
                                   "Right hand, hook."
                                   "Two jabs . . ."
            He stopped—
                    "Always use yuh reach.
                            Use yuh reach.
                    Boxin' is about yuh reach.

                                   Boxin' is all about thinkin'
                                            —it's like chess."

"Have you evuh written a book?" Benny asks me,
                                   as we did the moves around the floor,
                                            right hand,
                            upper cut,
                    weavin',
            double-weave right hand,
       hook—
            He continued—
                    "I was watchin' Oprah yesterday, and I got an idea for a book.
                       It would be called
                            I Can Walk in Your Shoes, and You Can Walk in Mines."
       —Two jabs.
                    "I Can Walk in Your Shoes, and You Can Walk in Mines,"
                                   he said with emphasis.

Benny's book would be about rich and poor.
            We are all interested in that which we identify as our ultimate opposite.

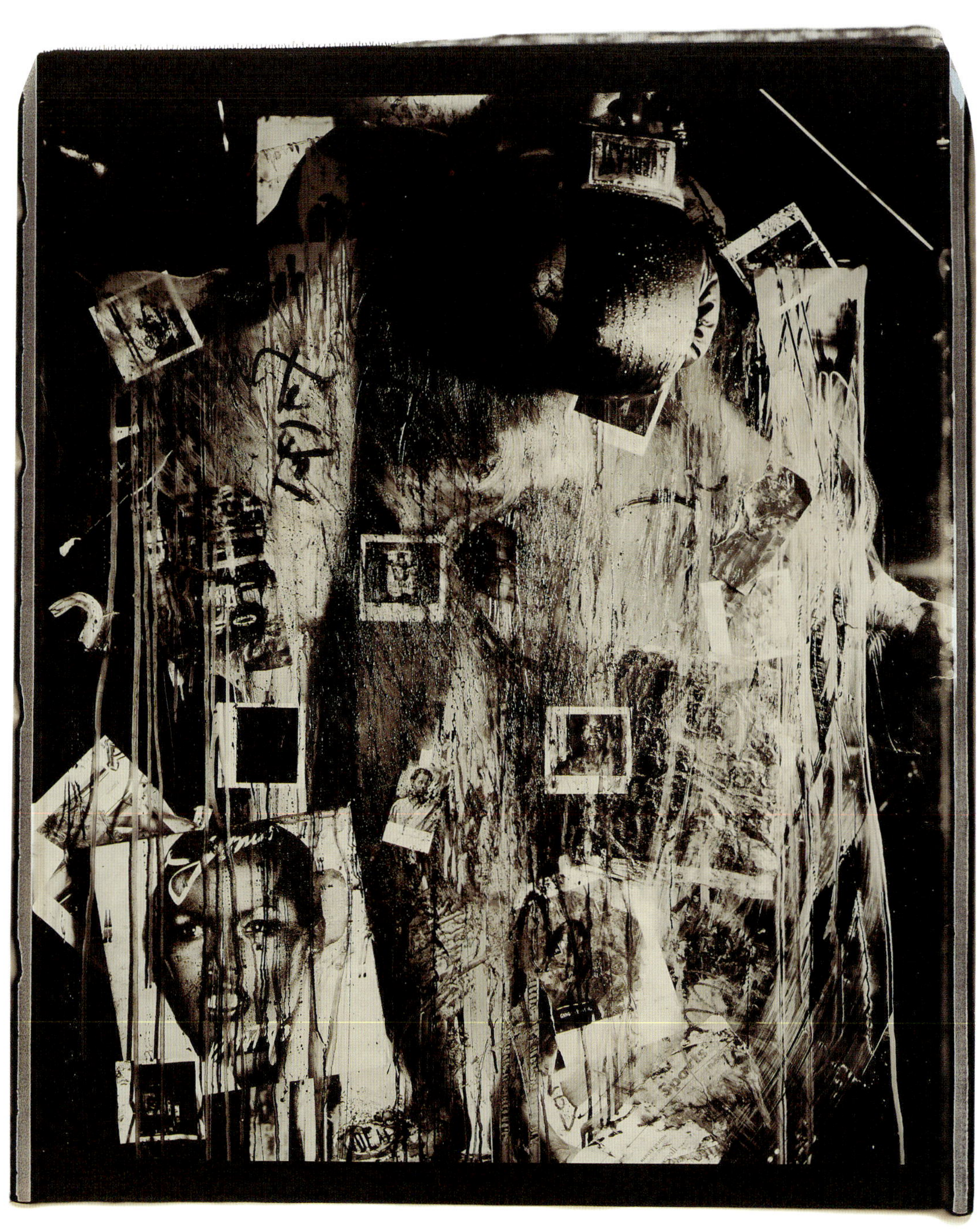

X

Why is Lyle the

      whoosh,

      the

      pow   pow   pow   pow   pow?

Why is he the wailing face of the boxer
And also the wailing face of the diva?

    Thank you thank you thank you ladies and gentlemen.
    And now I'd like to sing a tune that was written especially for me.
    It's titled "Strange Fruit," I hope you'll like it.

        Southern trees bear a strange fruit,
        Blood on the leaves and blood at the root,
        Black body swinging in the Southern breeze,
        Strange fruit hanging from the poplar trees. . . .

Presumably the lynching had an audience, just as Billie singing the song has an audience.
    The boxer, the Billie, the lynching.
        They are all spectacles, all racial spectacles.

        Hush now, don't explain
        I know you're asking
        I'm glad you're back
        Don't explain

Why is Lyle both the suffering boxer, and the committed, with conviction,
        so much conviction, convicted, singing Billie?

Like I said, when I asked him, "Why?" he got that sort of surprised, engaged look on his face,
    That
    reach,
    and said,
      "Well, what do you think?"

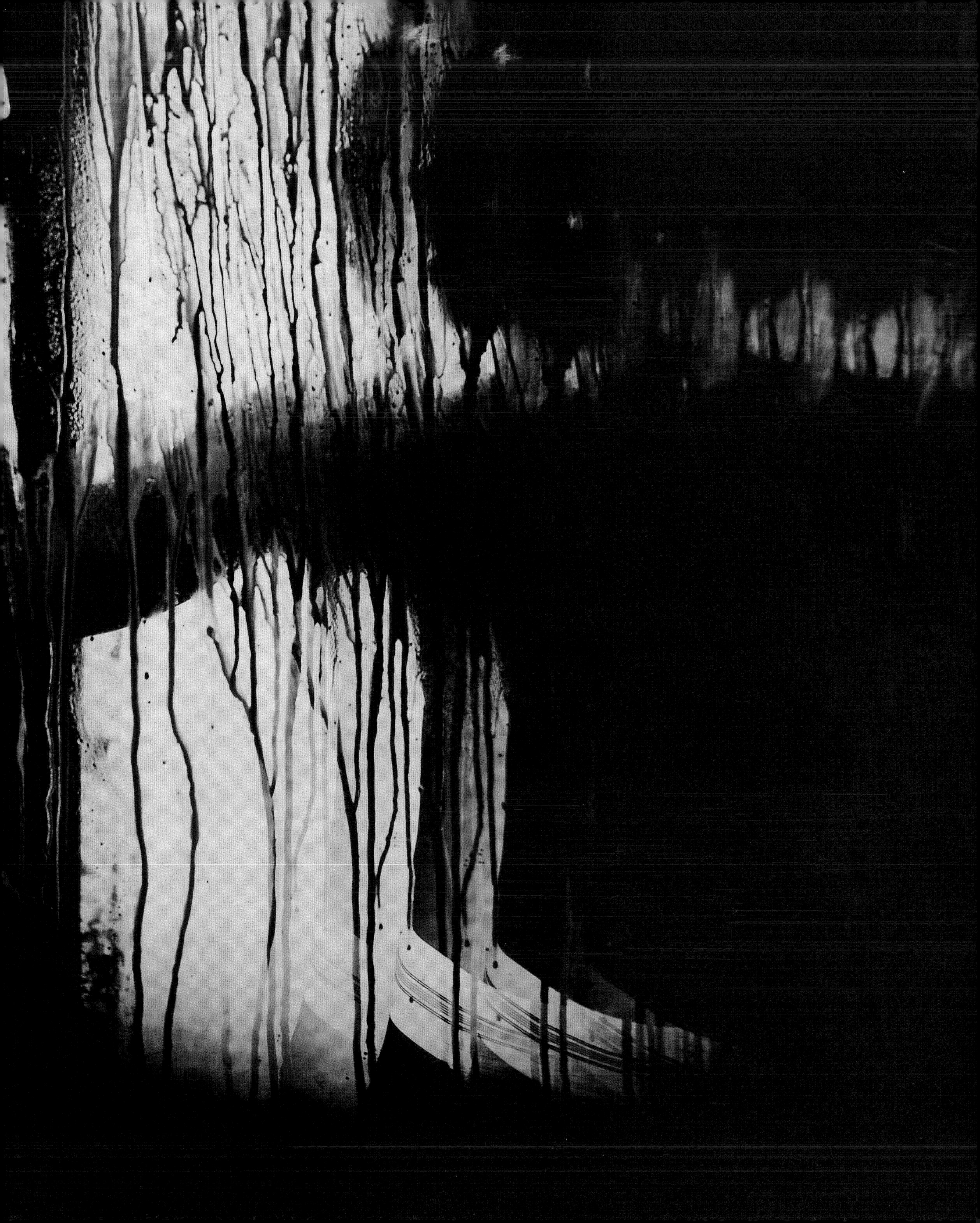

I think the boxer is the one who takes the punch and the singer is the one who heals the bloody wound—even as she herself is bruised. I think the singer is the one who has to sing even if her face is dripping blood, and the boxer is the one who has to box even if he would rather sing to you—oh, how much he loves you. I think the boxer is the one who has to slip out of the grip, even as he would like to stay in the grip. And I think by nightfall the singer is a man, because the world was tough as nails for a black woman.

I think the singer is the boxer the morning after the fight who still has to sing because the audience did not get enough of the fight, watching beaten black bodies, the insatiable audience, wondering if the singer was so high she might fall down on stage in the middle of a tune. And just because they paid to get in, do they have any idea what price the boxer, what price the singer pays?

(I can't think of a better subtitle for what Lyle does than Benny's title—
"I Can Walk in Your Shoes, and You Can Walk in Mines."

"Mines"—yes. "Mines." Yes, "mines." Lyle walks in mines.
Land mines, gold mines—but do most of us?)

And I think you are the audience if you only walk in your shoes and can never walk in mines. And I think if you can walk out of your shoes and can walk in mines then you become a boxer and a singer too. And I think the boxer is Daddy and the singer is Mama and Sugar is the nightfall and the mourning break. I think . . .

Enough about what I think,
I could go on forever about what I think.
You don't look at Lyle's work to learn what I think.

The sentence ends
Only because there is a period and no words.
Beauty can never be stated in a sentence with a beginning middle and end.
Beauty could only possibly be in a run-on sentence
Like the horn in Billie's voice or the blood flying off the boxer's face.

When I am lookin' for Lyle
And lookin' for beauty in the way he dares to put his own face in a picture that is not his face,
I am lookin' for the run-on face that runs into his face.
I am lookin' for the blood that runs between his faces.
The blood of the boxer that runs into the blood of Billie.

I am lookin' for beauty
In his mirror
The mirror that runs on and on and on and on . . .
I am looking at his life sentence.
The sentence that places him not here not there,
But in between here and there.

I am longing to see that Daddy
That Lyle is lookin' for.

I am lookin' for Lyle
Because his melancholy is the unfinished business of his mourning.

Oh how,
I am longing for that Daddy
Who could ever possibly
Be as beautiful as
The look,
For Daddy.

Anna Deavere Smith
Taormina, Italy – June 2002

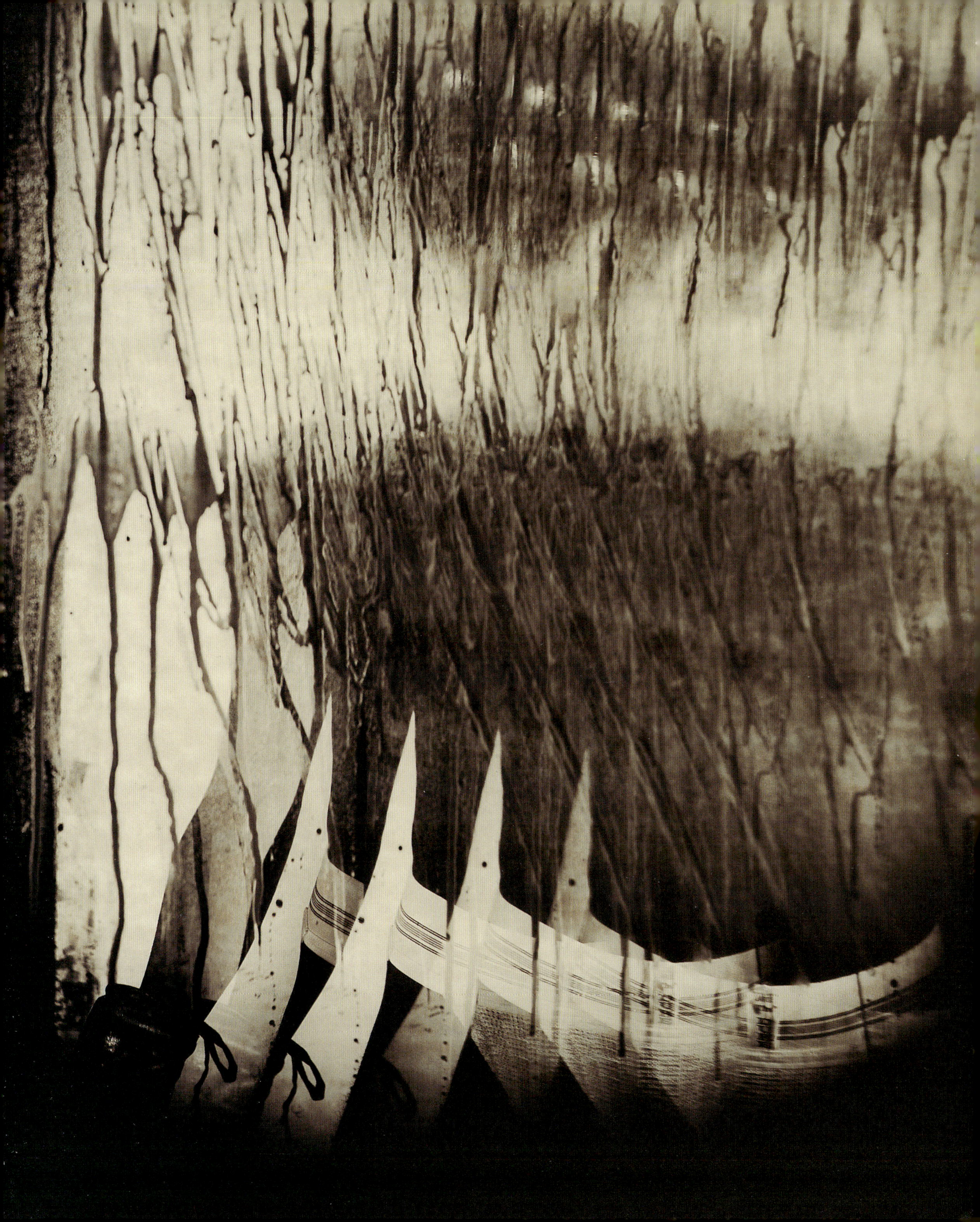

Lyle Ashton Harris was born in the Bronx and raised in New York City and Dar Es Salaam, Tanzania. His work has been exhibited internationally, including at the Guggenheim Museum, the Whitney Museum of American Art, the Corcoran Gallery of Art, the Walker Art Center, the Institute of Contemporary Arts in London, the Kunsthalle Basel, and the Centre d'Art Contemporain in Geneva. His work is in numerous public collections, including the Whitney Museum of American Art, the Walker Art Center, the Los Angeles County Museum of Art, and the Museum of Contemporary Art, Los Angeles. During 2000 and 2001, he was a fellow at the American Academy in Rome. He is represented by CRG Gallery in New York.

Anna Deavere Smith is an actor, director, playwright, and teacher whose work combines the journalistic technique of interviewing her subjects with the art of interpreting their words through performance. She was awarded a fellowship from the MacArthur Foundation in 1996 and has won numerous awards for her work in the theater, including two Obies and two Tony nominations. She is a tenured professor at New York University with an appointment to the Tisch School of the Arts and an affiliation with New York University School of Law, as well as being the founding director of the Institute on the Arts and Civic Dialogue, dedicated to creating art for social change. She serves as Artist-in-Residence at MTV Networks.

List of Works

IN ORDER OF APPEARANCE

Cover:
Memoirs of Hadrian #19
Monochromatic dye diffusion transfer print (Polaroid), 24 x 20 in.
Private collection, New York

Frontispiece:
Je ne sais quoi #5
Monochromatic dye diffusion transfer print (Polaroid), 24 x 20 in.
Collection of Gregory Miller

Billie #19
Monochromatic dye diffusion transfer print (Polaroid), 24 x 20 in.
Collection of Peter Norton

Memoirs of Hadrian #1
Monochromatic dye diffusion transfer print (Polaroid), 24 x 20 in.
Courtesy of Baldwin Gallery, Aspen

Billie #23
Monochromatic dye diffusion transfer print (Polaroid), 24 x 20 in.
Collection of the artist

Billie #22
Monochromatic dye diffusion transfer print (Polaroid), 24 x 20 in.
Courtesy of CRG Gallery, New York

Billie #2
Monochromatic dye diffusion transfer print (Polaroid), 24 x 20 in.
Collection of Peter Norton

Better Days #2
Monochromatic dye diffusion transfer print (Polaroid), 24 x 20 in.
Courtesy of Baldwin Gallery, Aspen

Je ne sais quoi #3
Monochromatic dye diffusion transfer print (Polaroid), 24 x 20 in.
Collection of Claudia Cisneros

Memoirs of Hadrian #16
Monochromatic dye diffusion transfer print (Polaroid), 24 x 20 in.
Courtesy of CRG Gallery, New York

Memoirs of Hadrian #26
Monochromatic dye diffusion transfer print (Polaroid), 24 x 20 in.
Collection of Ann and Ron Pizzuti

Memoirs of Hadrian #17
Monochromatic dye diffusion transfer print (Polaroid), 24 x 20 in.
Courtesy of CRG Gallery, New York

Memoirs of Hadrian #23
Monochromatic dye diffusion transfer print (Polaroid), 24 x 20 in.
Courtesy of CRG Gallery, New York

Billie #21
Monochromatic dye diffusion transfer print (Polaroid), 24 x 20 in.
Whitney Museum of American Art
Purchase, with funds from the Photography Committee 2002.563

Memoirs of Hadrian #1 (detail)
Monochromatic dye diffusion transfer print (Polaroid), 24 x 20 in.
Courtesy of Baldwin Gallery, Aspen

Memoirs of Hadrian #32
Dye diffusion transfer print (Polaroid), 24 x 20 in.
Private collection, New York

Blue Billie
Dye diffusion transfer print (Polaroid), 24 x 20 in.
Courtesy of CRG Gallery, New York

Memoirs of Hadrian #19
Monochromatic dye diffusion transfer print (Polaroid), 24 x 20 in.
Private collection, New York

Memoirs of Hadrian #18
Monochromatic dye diffusion transfer print (Polaroid), 24 x 20 in.
Courtesy of CRG Gallery, New York

Memoirs of Hadrian #25
Monochromatic dye diffusion transfer print (Polaroid), 24 x 20 in.
Private collection, New York

For Joella

Acknowledgements

Lyle Ashton Harris would like to acknowledge the following individuals for their contribution to the production of the series of photographs from which the images in this book have been selected: Isabelle Lumpkin, art direction; Michael Alsondo, hair and makeup.

Special thanks to the following individuals for their support:
Anna Deavere Smith; Harley Baldwin and Richard Edwards - Baldwin Gallery;
Robert Crane and Shirley Muñoz; Tim Hailand; Rudean Leinaeng; Thomas Allen Harris;
Maripol; Sipho Sokudela; John Reuter and Ben Fraser - 20 x 24 Polaroid Studio;
David Adamson; Christopher Burke; Tommy Gear; Gregory Miller; Qingcai Zhang, M.D.;
Kevin Walz; Carla Chammas, Richard Desroche, Glenn McMillan, Glen Baldridge,
Alex Dodge, and Brian Monte - CRG Gallery, New York.

All works were executed at the 20 x 24 Polaroid Studio, New York, New York.

Published by Gregory R. Miller & Company
62 Cooper Square, New York, New York 10003

in collaboration with

CRG Gallery
535 West 22nd Street, New York, New York 10011